Job Shadowing

Techniques to Get Maximum Impact from the Experience

By Kyle Richards

Table of Contents

Introduction

Job shadowing is an experience that is very eye-opening and a powerful tool in the use of career exploration. Whether you are in high school, in college, a recent graduate, middle aged, or even into your last few years of employment, job shadowing can be an incredible tool to assist you in finding the right path for you.

Sometimes job shadowing is used within a company to cross train employees on other tasks, and other times it is used as a leadership development tool for a company. A company may also use job shadowing to test to see if a particular employee would be a good match for a lateral type job position change.

When I was going through a phase of career search myself, this was an assignment that was given to me in a college class. When first learning of the assignment, it sounded pretty lame to me, to be honest. But since I actually had to DO the experience to pass the class, I was SHOCKED to see what a life changing experience job shadowing truly was!

Keep reading to learn how you too can gain the most from a job shadow opportunity.

What is Job Shadowing?

What exactly is job shadowing? In a nutshell, it's a way for students or older workers contemplating a career change to see the day-to-day operations that a job entails. One example is an education major student, who might shadow a principal or assistant principal throughout the day or for a portion of the day. The job shadower follows the mentor for a few hours or days to see what a particular job may entail. But there's more to job shadowing than that simple explanation. Job shadowing provides a far richer experience than reading a job description or doing an informational interview during which an employee describes his or her work. Job shadowing allows the observer to see and understand the nuances of a particular job.

By following someone while on the job, it allows someone (when time permits) to ask more specific questions. Sometimes these questions may be fueled by what the person sees on the job itself, and it might be a question that had never been thought about prior to the experience.

Job shadowing can be a very effective tool in the selection of a career, whether one is a student, middle aged, or older searching for a career change.

It may help a person to decide if a particular job field is the right one for them. Sometimes job shadowing is the required curriculum for a college or university program, such as nursing or teaching. Doing job shadowing independently, meaning apart from a school program, also has merit. It may save someone from having to repurpose themselves or switch careers mid-stream. Job shadowing can be described as due diligence for the career seeker. It can also become a gateway to getting hired.

Higher education is very expensive these days, and it's important to really know your target before potentially wasting time and money on a career choice that will ultimately not work out.

Statistics point to the trend that a person will have several different careers in their lifetime, and that many will not even be working remotely in the field they originally received education for.

I know of several cases where expensive mistakes could have been avoided by a simple job shadowing experience. One was a woman in cosmetology school who was very close to graduating before realizing she was allergic to common chemicals used in the industry and that she simply couldn't tolerate it physically. Someone early on should have recommended an allergy test for some of these chemicals before she spent thousands of dollars she was not obligated to pay on a school that gave her no viable career.

A second case was a high school graduate who had never worked on a vehicle in his life and went to a very specialized mechanic school out of state. It was a top of the line school in the field, and he chose this career based upon wages earned, job opportunities in the area he wanted to live, and other factors that were solid reasons for choosing this field. He got there and was close to graduating when he realized he had zero natural aptitude for the field and he despised the work. He worked for 6 months in the industry, jumping from job to job because his skills were so poor he couldn't hold a job. He hated every minute of it and was thousands of dollars in debt. A relevant job shadowing situation may have exposed his disinterest and lack of natural inclination for this career path.

There are thousands of people with college degrees that are simply not relevant to the career choice they really wanted. Maybe those degrees sound great, but in reality, there are no jobs that fit. Yet, the debt is there. These as well as various other scenarios happen all the time, and it is tragic. Many could be avoided with a really good job shadowing experience.

As far as students go, job shadowing saturates a student into the work world, so each can glean information first-hand concerning careers and job skills. It can give rich and unique experiences that are truly one of a kind to those who participate. It helps students get a more concrete concept of real options for their lives in a meaningful way. It helps them see the goal, thus inspiring them to work at their studies, creating a vital link between success and education. It helps them own their dreams, goals and aspirations for a better future.

Job shadowing activities are most successful when they are integrated into a specific required class. The standards, preparation, and follow-up must be part of a curriculum. A job shadow activity takes several hours from the workday and school day. Therefore, students should complete career assessments and research careers to help them narrow down career areas of interest.

Job shadowing is helpful in these applications:

1. Helps students "test drive" a career.

2. Provides an environment in which they can network with professionals.

3. Demonstrates the connections between academics and careers and helps students learn by making their classwork more relevant.

4. Identifies the skills, qualities, training, and education needed to succeed on the job.

5. Builds community partnerships between schools and businesses that enhance the educational experience of all students.

6. Introduces students to the requirements of professions and

industries to help them prepare to join the workforce of the 21st century.

7. Encourages an ongoing relationship between students and caring adults in their communities.

Hopefully by now you can see the benefit of participating in a job shadow experience in your own career search. In the next chapter, we'll be exploring ways to land a job shadow opportunity.

Procuring a Job Shadow Opportunity

Now is the time to try to procure a job shadow opportunity. You may want to consider doing several, at least one for the field of work you are considering. If it's a strong consideration, do at least 3 if possible.

Start by making a list. Write down the career fields you would like to job shadow, including careers that are closely related. Next, write down companies, non-profit organizations, or employers within that field in your city or town or nearby that you would be willing to drive to for a job shadow. You may need to do an internet or library search for this information.

Here's where we will explore two different approaches, one being for a larger corporation that may have a job shadowing program in place and the other for either smaller companies or non-profit organizations.

Asking a Non-Profit or Smaller Business

Draft a letter that includes the date and the name and address of the person you would like to shadow. If you don't know, then try addressing it to an HR department, public relations, or a similar position. If that person isn't the correct one, ask their recommendation for who to send it to. You may be able to find the information on that company's website.

In your letter, write an introductory paragraph about who you are, how you found them or were referred by them, the reason you are contacting them, and what you hope to gain in a job shadow situation for your career.

In your request, also give them the time frame you would like to job shadow. Examples might be a whole day, half a day, etc. Ask permission at the end of the job shadow to do an informational interview with them about the experience for 15–20 minutes. If they grant you that time, be sure to honor it and not go over!

Acknowledge to them that you realize you are asking a lot. Explain as quickly as possible why you believe job shadowing can help you in your career path and that any help they could offer you, you would be grateful for.

Thank them for their time reading your letter and consideration of your request. Let them know you will contact them in a week for their decision (make sure you follow up on this in 7 days). Give them your contact email and phone number so they can reach you if they have questions before they make a decision.

Send the letter by snail mail. Be aware that people are extremely busy, and if they do agree, it could be several weeks out before they can fit it into their schedules. If you are denied your request, don't take it personally, but thank them for their time and ask if they might be able to recommend someone else in the field who they might be willing to refer you to. If they agree, ask them their availability, then book it.

Write a follow-up thank you letter to this person for their time and consideration, whether or not they gave you a job shadow opportunity. If they did, express your excitement of the upcoming time with them.

Contacting a Large Corporation That Has an Existing Job Shadow Program

If you are a student or alumnus, talk to the representative at your college career services department. Ask them to contact the corporation on your behalf requesting information about the job shadow program requirements or referral process.

If you are an individual, contact the HR department to request the information yourself.

Once you have received their procedures, follow them exactly.

Virtual Job Shadowing

Because we live in a digital world, it's important to keep in mind that not all job shadowing has to be physical. There is now an option called virtual job shadowing where career candidates can do reality-based career exploration.

On virtualjobshadow.com, virtual job shadowing of a climate scientist who looks at global change issues and how it affects humans, other species, and the earth is possible. Such an individual may make maps, movies, and visual images that help people be more climate smart. Video images, transcriptions about the career, and questions and answers are found on the site. In the video, climate scientist Ned Garnier explains things such as the fact that probes and ocean thermometers as well as other tools help people understand earth processes better, adapt to those processes, and remain safe in doing so.

Virtual job shadowing of other professions is also possible on this site, such as a sustainability architect, an operating room nurse, and a mechanical engineer.

One government site gives a list of 25 sites where one can complete virtual job shadowing. Some of them are private, and some are governmental sites.

There are even YouTube videos on job shadowing. One involves a veterinarian and owner of an animal hospital. He explains his job and the tools he needs. "Every day is different in some way because animals, like people, are all a little different." He stresses that a person needs to have great people skills and problem-solving skills. In the 1 minute and 43 second video, he tells about the career requirements for a veterinary career. The video shows him examining and treating a dog while his assistant helps to hold him. There is a voice over where he narrates and provides information.

You can also ask friends and family for recommendations. You could even post a request on Facebook for job shadow opportunities, you just never know what may turn up.

Got My Job Shadow Booked – What Next?

Congratulations, you've got the job shadow opportunity booked. Now what? Research is one key. Research the organization beforehand to get a feel for the corporate culture, dress code, and etiquette. Research the profession and have some knowledge of the occupation and industry. Try not to ask anything that should be common knowledge; learn as much as you can in advance so you can target your questions toward relevant information.

Ask for the agenda. Ask your mentor for a schedule to help you prepare. If the visit includes lunch, research the dress code, menu, and other specifics so you'll know what to order and how to behave and dress. If the visit includes sitting in on meetings or accompanying your host to other official functions, learn as much about these proceedings as you can.

Compile a list of questions (sample ones later) well in advance of your job shadow day, and rehearse them. Determine what you need to know to help you prepare you for career success and to decide if this is the right profession for you. You might not have to time to ask every question on your list, so determine which ones are the most important to you so you can seek opportunities to discuss them early in the day. Also, prepare for the host's questions. They'll likely ask you to tell them about yourself and why you're interested in the profession.

Arrive on time. During the day, do your best not to get in your mentor's way. It might be good to ask early about what they need of you during this process. If you are one who talks quite a bit, be sure to curb this. You want to be as considerate as possible to their needs too.

What questions should you ask? Here are a few to consider:

- What type of skills, education, and training do you need for this career?

- How has this career field changed since you started in it?

- What advice do you have for somebody considering this career?

- How did you know this was the right career for you?

- Are you passionate about your career? If so, why?

- What do you see as the biggest changes that have happened in this career field?

- How does your employer differ from their competitors?

- What do you like most about your job?

- What do you like least about your job?

- Can you describe a typical day at your job?

- How much are you required to work outside normal business hours?

- What are some of the biggest challenges you face in your job?

- How much does this career and job affect your personal life?

- What's the most valuable reward you receive from this job?

- What's the most valuable lesson you've learned – about this career, your job, or life in general?

- What's the most important advice you have for someone just starting out in this career?

- What type of websites and other tools do you use to stay current with your career/profession?

- Do you expect the workplace to change much over the next five years?

- What is the employment outlook for this career field?

- Is there anything else that I have not seen today or that we have not talked about that you think is important for me to know as I continue my quest for the ideal career for me?

- Is there anything else you think I should know?

Send a thank you note to your mentor for the job shadow opportunity immediately after it's done.

While it's still fresh, sit down and write notes about the experience, answers to your questions, and your impressions and feelings about it. Sleep on it, and do this again the next day. Do it again a week later. See if there's a common theme between these notes, and see what remains the strongest information. If it brought more questions to you, do further research to get those answered.

A Few Specific Industry Job
Shadowing Tips & Experiences

In this next section, we'll be looking at a few industry specific tips and questions that will be useful to those fields. Some of these will be people sharing their real life experiences of job shadowing within their own careers.

When you go to do your own job shadowing, consider any specialized questions you should be asking that are industry specific.

Nursing

Ask your mentor about his or her own career choices and how they came to the conclusion that nursing was the field they wanted to enter as opposed to another health specialty in the health care occupation. For example, you could ask questions such as: "What satisfaction do you gain from nursing that you don't believe you could have gotten from being a physician?" "During your clinical rotations, what specialty areas did you enjoy the most and why?" "Have you thought about pursuing an advanced nursing degree to become a nurse practitioner, physician's assistant, or clinical specialist?"

Examine the procedures they use to perform specific clinical protocols, such as medical injection or intravenous medication administration, intubation, respiratory assessment or catheter insertion. Ask how they gained the skills they needed for difficult procedures and how long that process took before they were adept at doing these tasks.

Pose specific questions about working in various health care settings, such as the benefits of working in a hospital versus a long-term medical facility or nursing home. If they have experience working in a physician's office, ask questions about the private, one-on-one patient interaction versus the opportunity to provide care to several different patients in a facility setting. Ask them to share their perspective on working in faith-based hospitals versus community hospitals, if they have that kind of background.

Discuss the difficulties or challenges they meet as a co-worker of a health care team that is made up of doctors, charge nurses, nurse aides, and other staff positions, such as laboratory assistants and patient care technicians. Ask questions about hands-off procedures, shift change reviews, communication, and related topics.

One Austin nurse pursued her LVN first, and then years later decided to get on the fast track to earn her RN. She prefers to remain anonymous, but explained that she kept working at the same job at a state institution where the elderly, developmentally disabled, adult, and child clients are housed, while working to advance to RN status.

She recalled how she attended Austin Community College's (ACC) Mobility Track, which is for those who want to get their RN in one year instead of two. On ACC's website, it indicates that this accelerated track is designed for people who already have an LVN or students with prior healthcare experience. At any rate, this particular nurse explained how she knew the professional requirements of a nursing job and that when she did job shadowing, she learned the job differently while shadowing an experienced RN before becoming one herself.

This anonymous real-life nurse stated that she had to do clinical rotations while working on her RN credentials. These are also a type of job shadowing, except it allows for some hands-on experience, similar to an apprenticeship.

She stated unequivocally that she found her ideal career. "It's good helping people and seeing them get well. I enjoy taking care of people."

Another nurse, who works for Austin's St. David's Healthcare System, referred to her job shadowing experience as orientation. "It lasted a long time," she recalled.

Questions worth asking the person one is shadowing if one is considering trying to job shadow in nursing on their own might include the following:

1. How did you know for sure that nursing was a career that you would enjoy and be able to stick with for the long-term?

2. What, if anything, was your second choice of a career, and why did nursing inch to top spot over that career?

3. What do you get out of nursing that you might not have gotten out of another career?

4. What are some non-clinical ways that you could use your RN credentials if you ever choose to switch from patient care?

Also choose questions from the general list that are applicable to you that you are curious about.

Probation Officers / Law Enforcement

Probation officers are of vital important to the criminal justice system. They help monitor offenders that are put on probation, set rehab plans, and bring accountability to offenders ensuring they are keeping up their terms of probation and are not a threat. Job shadowing will allow to you see exactly what this career involves, and provides opportunity to ask questions to see if this career is the right one for you.

What to Expect

If you shadow a probation officer you may want to ask about tasks that are routine for them. How many offenders they see on average daily, how they track their progress, or set their schedules. You might want to see how much time they spend at their desk, or in the field, and about their own safety and well-being in this position. By gaining an overall picture you'll get a more accurate sense of this career.

How to Prepare

Ask the probation officer about the education and training necessary to step into this field of work. Ask if there are any state specific requirements in your state in addition to national standards. Find out if there are any age limitations.

When choosing a career, long-term career satisfaction is a prime concern. Ask what they dislike and like about their jobs, and ask for some specifics. Find out what their level of personal satisfaction is towards their career, and what they wished someone would have told them when they were considering it as a career.

Worth Your While

With any career choice, personal satisfaction is only part of the puzzle. A delicate series of question, yet necessary is that of pay scale. You might ask what average starting salaries are in the state, raises and how those are usually dispensed. You might want to ask about career advancement options, how those are earned and how long they usually take. Make sure you don't ask how much they make!

The purpose of job shadowing is to learn as much as possible about a particular career so you know if it is something you can see yourself doing in the future. Shadowing at a police department can orient you to the types of duties you might be performing as an officer of the law or as a support professional who works in the police department. Come prepared with a list of questions to ask so you can get the most from your job shadow experience.

Job Duties

First and foremost, you want to know what kind of duties you can expect to be performing in various positions. If possible, interview different people in the department about their responsibilities, roles and duties. This gives you an idea of where you would most like to see yourself working. Speak to a beat cop, a secretary, a police chief, a detective, or other individuals available about their roles, if possible. Talking to different people can help give you a well-rounded view of the world of law enforcement.

Job Benefits/Drawbacks

You want to uncover what different personnel see as the pros and cons of their careers. Each role most likely will have very different positive and negatives specific to their positions.

Job Preparation

Ask about the required steps a person must take to get into the position you desire at a police department, and about where someone can obtain that schooling or training. Ask what standards need to be met, perhaps age and ability issues.

Chiropractor

Baker Chiropractic has Pflugerville and South Austin office locations in Texas. Dr. Baker explained that when he opened his practice about 15 years ago, patients thought he was too young to be in practice. However, before spending three years in a busy Houston area practice, he obtained his credentials at Texas Chiropractic College in Pasadena, Texas.

When he talked about job shadowing in his profession, he mentioned how most such candidates were already certain they wished to become chiropractors. As he explained it, students who job shadow a chiropractor will get to see some of the intricacies of the practice, such as the use of diagnostic and treatment-oriented equipment.

Some relevant questions that such a student might ask while job shadowing such a professional are included below:

1. What percentage of the time do you spend on your feet?

2. How much time per day do you dedicate to reviewing X-rays?

3. What are the pros and cons of having a private practice?

4. What were some of the pros and cons of working in a clinic other than your own?

5. How long does it take to get a good customer base?

6. What do you think the outlook for this profession is?

Physical Therapy

A physical therapist, Doctor Patrice Moreland, explained how she job shadowed while considering a career in physical therapy. She said becoming a chiropractor was a second choice. To help her decide, she did some research and then job shadowed before applying for a doctorate program in physical therapy at Dallas' UT Southwestern.

She had taught science for two and a half years in the Dallas Independent School District in an inner city middle school. While she was still teaching, she job shadowed at an outpatient clinic and at a nursing home.

She waited until summer break and then called her personnel department at both places and asked for a job shadowing opportunity. "It's not an uncommon thing for people to call and want to job shadow." She set a certain time to visit each place for her job shadowing appointment.

At a privately owned outpatient clinic, she shadowed an older gentleman physical therapist while he visited with two elderly clients. One patient helped him with intake, like a clerical person. She recalled thinking that the profession could probably be carried out better with clerical assistance.

She also job shadowed at a skilled nursing home with an elderly population at a variety of levels. She said that's when she realized that she liked working with the elderly. "I felt very comfortable with that population."

The reason she knew about the job shadowing experience when considering a career shift from teaching to physical therapy is that she also did it when she was younger. She earned her B.S. in biology in 2004, but job shadowed at a clinic while in undergraduate college. "I liked patient care, so I wanted to explore a field where I could be involved in patient care all day, every day."

She said she would recommend that anyone considering becoming a physical therapist try shadowing in more than one setting. "That's because they may observe a therapist in a nursing home and it may turn them off because it doesn't appeal to them in that setting, but therapists work in different settings, and one might work better than another."

Moreland worked for three years in a skilled nursing facility after obtaining her degree, passing her licensure exam, and doing her clinical, which was another type of job shadowing.

Recently, she started operating her own physical therapy company, where she carries her own patient load and visits patients in their homes. Her company operates under the name Patrice Moreland, DPT.

Moreland shared her idea of some critical questions that a job shadowing candidate in her field consider asking the person they shadow, as follows:

- How many patients do they see a day?

- What is the paperwork load like?

Education

One online student, who is working on a Master's in Education at Liberty University, recalled that she was not given the option to job shadow or not. The requirement came along with her coursework. As she explained it, her professor gave them specific directions and a template to fill out for the job shadowing experience. Nonetheless, she still recalls that she had some flexibility in terms of questions to ask.

She asked several questions of her own choosing and would recommend that anyone seeking to enter the field do the same. They follow below:

1. What kind of paperwork do you have to do?

2. Do you think union membership is necessary?

3. How many hours outside of school hours do you work?

4. Do you work weekends?

5. What part of the job do you like the most?

6. What part of the job do you dislike?

7. How can one tell which age group or grades are best for them?

8. How much time do you spend on your feet every day?

Special Education

This same student had to job shadow special education teachers, although she was not a special education major. She stated that this experience taught her that she was definitely not called to this special population, made her appreciate the teachers who dedicate themselves to such students, and provided her with tools for those students who may be placed in a regular classroom, which is where she was hoping to find herself assigned.

Still, she had some questions for the seasoned special education teachers whom she shadowed. Some of them follow below:

1. Do you think it's important to get training in restraint procedures?

2. What are your strategies for managing multiple individual education plans (IEP's)?

3. Is there such a thing as a student you can't handle?

4. Would you like to work with the general school population?

5. What about teaching this special population appeals to you?

6. How much time do you spend on your feet every day?

Journalism

A reporter found her true sweet spot when she job shadowed a reporter to see what the job entails. Today, she mentors others with the same goal. As she explained it, her desire was to see if she was cut out to be a hard news reporter. A hard news reporter may have to deal with a good number of formal and serious topics and events. Business, politics, and international news falls in this category.

After shadowing a journalist who had to go out and cover such news and then write newspaper articles about it, she realized that although this person showed true passion for that line of work, she didn't feel cut out for it.

Her next job shadow experience involved shadowing a features writer. Feature articles may cover topics such as lifestyle, money, career, relationships, or the arts.

When this student was attending Southwest Texas State University, she had to cover both kinds of news and write both hard and feature articles. She also had to write broadcast segments for hard and "soft" news.

Writing hard news always took her longer, and she sometimes became a bit down in the dumps while interviewing or going to such events and then writing about them. Besides job shadowing that type of news reporter, class requirements along the same lines told her that she might not be cut out to be a hard news reporter.

What she decided to do was get through those class requirements the best way she could. Then she went to see Dan Rather, who spoke at the Texas Book Festival in 2012 at the State Capital building. Rather had a long-standing career as a news anchor on CBS evening news. He spoke of hard news with such passion that she knew that she didn't have the same drive to cover hard news.

After this experience, she decided that although she was majoring in broadcasting because she had once wanted to be a Barbara Walters or a Dan Rather, she would become a print journalist instead.

While she cites several experiences as contributing to her final career decision, such as seeing Dan Rather speak, completing hard news stories, and job shadowing, she states that she found the perfect career and is still in love with the work that she does as a feature writer for a newspaper. She said that while she didn't get all the insight she needed in time to change the concentration of her degree, she did have an opportunity to take more print journalism classes.

She explained how she arrived at a decision she could live with by stating, "A hard news reporter may report on the number of bicycle accidents and fatalities that occurred over a period of time, while a feature news reporter will report on the new bicycle lanes and bike storage capabilities tied to the city's transit system. Job shadowing helped me to distinguish which type of news appealed to me the most. I could see myself doing this type of news for a couple of decades, if possible."

The reporter thought it important for anyone considering such a career look closely at the type of jobs one could obtain with a journalism degree.

- News Anchor

- News Correspondent

- Print Journalist

- War Correspondent

- Print News Editor

- Assignment Editor

- Broadcast News Analysts

- Radio Announcer

- Public Service Announcer

Some questions the reporter felt were important for a person to ask if they are considering a career in communications or journalism, whether they know what specialization they intend to pursue or not, follow below:

1. Do you prefer writing lengthy pieces or short pieces?

2. Would you prefer that your job involves more writing of news or reporting of news?

3. Are you good at spontaneous banter, which might be required in broadcasting?

4. Do you like being live on camera with little notice?

5. Do you know how to create spontaneous ad lib and short news copy?

6. Are you more articulate or more fastidious about typographical and grammar errors?

7. Do you like writing short jingles or thoughtful, measured news articles?

8. Do you mind spending an incredible amount of time at a computer?

9. Does the work of personalities like Dan Rather/Barbara Walters/Katie Couric/Walter Cronkite/David Brinkley/Peter Jennings appeal to you? If so, what part of their job appeals

to you the most?

10. Do you like to conduct interviews, do investigations, and research?

11. Would you be able to switch to another field in communications after several years if you wanted to without going back to school for more training?

12. Do you notice errors in documents that dictate their need for revising or editing? Could this inclination mean someone would make a good editor?

13. Do you find yourself out covering news or conducting interviews during inclement weather? If so, what percentage of the time?

14. Could you see yourself working in a foreign country as a correspondent?

15. Could you see yourself working as a war correspondent in a war zone? If so, what could be the plus side of such work?

16. How good do you have to be at pulling together information from several sources?

17. What would you offer as a tip for keeping reporting unbiased, objective, and ethical?

18. What are your views on protecting news sources who wish to remain anonymous?

Librarian

Edward Young, a librarian with the Round Rock Public Library, explained how their volunteers get an opportunity to shadow a librarian to casually observe and experience the job so that they may be able to decide if it's a career or job they'd like to have.

Young specified that volunteers and new hires have to shadow someone for a while until they are released to perform the necessary tasks on their own. "They'll follow us for a few hours while we're working," he explained. He went on to elaborate that they have to show them how shelving and other job tasks are done.

One librarian with a Master's in Library Science and 15 years of experience as a librarian shared that the internet has impacted the need for librarians. She also said library staff were reduced across the board when the economy tanked in 2008-2009. She also indicated that in the Greater Dallas Texas area, only North Texas State and Texas Women's University offer Master's in Library Science degrees. She said many librarians will not hire someone with a Bachelor's in Library Science degree.

She stated that even public schools have reduced the number of librarians to the point where one librarian may float to two or three different schools, especially at the elementary level.

"It's hit the whole profession." The whole industry has been affected. She said she didn't do job shadowing when she was considering becoming a librarian, but that she has seen instances where a library science major has come to their location to gain more insights into what the job entails. Her idea for some questions to ask when shadowing a librarian follow below:

1. What's the job situation like?

2. Is there much turnover in the profession, or do librarians tend to stay on their jobs until retirement?

3. What can someone do with a Bachelor's in Library Science besides work in a library?

4. What can someone do with a Master's in Library Science besides work in a library?

5. Are new libraries/more branches needed in this market?

6. What does it take to become a director of a library system?

7. What does it take to become a branch supervisor?

8. What else can someone do in a library besides be a librarian?

Entrepreneur

A lot of people would love nothing more than to fire their boss, start their own business, and then ride into the sunset – on the way to the bank, of course. However, this can be a tricky situation, and it will require more than skills and a fervent hope to transition into a full-time business endeavor. Some entrepreneurs, who initially complain about the long hours they have to work on a job, balk when they discover that their own business may require even more work hours as well as more responsibility. This does not suggest that becoming an entrepreneur is out of reach. In fact, job shadowing someone in the field in which you are interested may have merit. Many entrepreneurs are happy to share their knowledge, but if you are to become a potential competitor for the same piece of pie, you may need to consider making a job shadow appointment in a different city. Incorporating it into a vacation trip or other travels might be a way to maximize the experience.

Should you decide to job shadow an entrepreneur, here are some things to consider:

1. Are you interested in a franchise or an independent business?

2. Will you be a partnership, corporation, or individually owned business?

3. Do you have sufficient start-up capital?

4. Do you have a business plan all sketched out?

If you feel ready to take the leap, job shadowing can equip you with more knowledge about your intended business. Try to take copious notes during your shadow day, both during the job shadowing and after. Also, have a list of questions for the person you are shadowing. Following are a few suggestions:

1. Is the time demand what you expected it to be, more than you expected, or less than you expected?

2. What surprises have you had since becoming a business owner?

3. How can you leverage the job skills you already have to work effectively in this business?

4. What, if anything, would you do differently from the way you did it?

5. What additional classes or training have you taken or would you take in order to run this business more effectively?

One key factor worthy of notice is that some franchises can give entrepreneurs an opportunity to start their own business using the blueprint already established. Many may require significant start-up cash, but the benefit is that the business owner doesn't have to start from scratch.

One enterprising couple, Paul and Lori Hogan, took advantage of a niche market opportunity by starting their non-medical home care business, which they named Home Instead Senior Care. Their business model has experienced so much success at filling in this special niche area for the elderly that they offer franchises. This particular model provides part-time or full-time live-in non-medical service. Personal care assistants hired to fill positions may find themselves doing light housework and offering assistance and companionship. The Hogans advertise that their franchisees receive training, ongoing support, and marketing support. The total investment to get on board with them is between $100,000-$150,000 plus a franchise fee of $45,000.

While there are similar franchises in this market, some don't stress their part in helping franchisees to acclimate.

Conclusion

As a conclusion to your job shadowing experience, take judicious notes including your feelings and impressions immediately after and a couple days and weeks after your job shadow.

If you are considering especially higher education in your career path, it would be wise to do at least 3 job shadows. Before you put a major money investment into a path, you want to get more than one person's opinion. By getting at least 3, you can look for common threads and see a wider range of options and opinions that can be very valuable information to you. Where one person might have missed or omitted information, another may fill in those gaps, plus they may give you more questions to ask during later job shadows.

It's also a wonderful networking and relationship building venue, and you just never know where it will lead.

Finally, remember this exercise is for your benefit. The more you put into it, the more you will get out of it. Learn and listen.

If you enjoyed this book or received value from it in any way, would you be kind enough to leave a review for it on Amazon? I would be so grateful. Thank you!

www.ingramcontent.com/pod-product-compliance
Lightning Source LLC
Chambersburg PA
CBHW020957180526
45163CB00006B/2408